PROGRAM
BOOK

compiled by

Pat Fittro

**STANDARD
PUBLISHING**
Cincinnati. Ohio

The Standard Publishing Company, Cincinnati, Ohio
A division of Standex International Corporation
©1995 by The Standard Publishing Company

ISBN 0-7847-0379-5

Contents

Christmas

Recitations

Exercises

Programs

Thanksgiving

Christmas Thought

Kay Hoffman

Soon Christmas will be over
  And the trimmings packed away;
With business then as usual
  We will go about our day.

But let us keep this thought in mind
  While Christmastime's still here.
Not to pack away the love,
  The kindness and good cheer.

The poor will still be with us
  And they'll need a helping hand.
The lonely will need cheer;
  From those who care and understand.

So have a merry Christmas
  Brimful of love and cheer
Then keep this self-same spirit
  To bless others through the year.

Peace, Joy & Love

Easy

Christmas Welcome

Iris Gray Dowling

We welcome you today.
I'm glad for all who came
To hear the words we say—
Merry Christmas to you all!

*(To the tune of "Happy Birthday To
You." These words could be sung
following the above welcome or at
the end of any program.)*

Merry Christmas to you,
Merry Christmas to you,
We're so glad you came today—
Merry Christmas to YOU!

All Year Long

Robert Colbert

All year long
  I've waited to say;
"Christ the Lord
  Is born this day!"

The Old, Old Story

Iris Gray Dowling

I have a cheerful message
  For every one of you.
Believe the old, old story—
  The Bible says it's true!
Receive what God has said—
  In His Word He speaks to YOU.

Gold

Iris Gray Dowling

A wise man brought a gift,
To give to Heaven's King.
He laid aside His crown—
That holy Son of God—
Who brought salvation down.

Jesus Loves Me

Lillian Robbins

Little children may not know
  All that grown-ups do.
But I know Jesus loves me,
  And Jesus loves you and you
    and you. *(Points to others.)*

Christmas Thoughts

Iris Gray Dowling

Not just another Christmas
  With gifts for all to see;
But thoughts of Christ, my Savior—
From sin He set me free.

Jesus' Birthday

Marion Schoeberlein

Happy birthday, Jesus,
  I'm so glad that YOU
Were born today for me
  And the whole world, too!

Christmas Hope

Iris Gray Dowling

Christmas bells should be rung,
  Pealing the message that Jesus
    taught.
Hear the songs that are sung,
  Telling the hope and the life He
    brought.

Tell the News

Iris Gray Dowling

There are songs to be sung;
There are bells to be rung;
There are hearts to be won;
Let us tell them of God's only Son.

Christmas Light

Iris Gray Dowling

Child of Bethlehem,
Who brought us Christmas light;
Open thou mine eyes,
And give me spiritual sight.

I'll Try It

Helen Kitchell Evans

My teacher was so positive
  That I could speak so clear
That I said, "I'll try it."
  My teacher is so dear.
So Merry Christmas everyone
  Have a Christmas filled with
    cheer.

So Dear!

Alta McLain

Happy birthday, Jesus!
  You are so dear to me,
For You came to make us happy.
  Your grace has set us free.

The Way

Alta McLain

Because God sent His Son to
    earth
  We can rejoice today
As we celebrate His birth.
  He came to show the way.

Christmas Love

Iris Gray Dowling

In the Babe of Bethlehem
  God sent His love to earth.
He brought salvation free—
  I'm glad for Jesus' birth.

The Christmas Story

Iris Gray Dowling

Did you know that at Christmas
    time
  There's a story that needs to be
    told?
Of a child from above, born on
    earth—
  With a message that never grows
    old.

God's Gift

Alta McLain

On Christmas Day we need to
    pray,
  To thank God for His Son,
The Perfect Gift, which all could
    share.
  He blesses everyone.

A Chosen Girl

Iris Gray Dowling

Mary was chosen by God,
  To mother His only begotten
  Son;
Favored above other girls,
  Her child was the Promised One.

When I'm Big

Helen Kitchell Evans

Someday when I'm big
  You will all recall
How I stood up here
  When I was quite small.

Happy Christmas one and all!

What Blessing!

Cora M. Owen

What blessings, joys and peace.
That never, never cease;
Because the Savior came.
All glory to His name!

The Guiding Star

Iris Gray Dowling

Wise men saw a brilliant star,
Guiding them from distance far.

Welcome

Dixie Phillips

We want to say we welcome you.
(Point to congregation.)
We are so glad you came
And to your video cameras,
We'd like to say the same:
"Welcome! Keep 'em rolling!"

Adorable

Dixie Phillips

I know I look adorable—
With my hair curled "just right,"
But tiny baby Jesus
Is the "real" star tonight!

Real Cute

Dixie Phillips

My mommy said I'm really cute,
My daddy said the same.
My minister said be sure to say:
"We're so glad you came!"
*(Cup hands around mouth, girl—
curtsy, boy—bow.)*

8

Medium

Real Loud

Dixie Phillips

My mommy said to speak "real
    loud,"
So my grandaddy could hear.
My daddy said to speak "real slow,"
So my words would be clear.
So, here I go to say my part:
I love baby Jesus with all my heart!

May It Be Done

Cora M. Owen

Oh, may the world echo the song,
  Which once the angels sang.
"Peace on the earth, good will to
  men."
  How joyfully it rang.

Oh, may the world behold the
  Christ,
  And own Him as the king;
Bring gifts to Him as those of yore,
  And yield Him everything.

Gladsome Story

Robert Colbert

Listen to the happy
Yuletide bells,
And the gladsome story
They always tell.

Christ is born!
Christ is born!
Let's welcome Him
This Christmas morn!

Renew Faith

Helen Kitchell Evans

Sometimes we get lost
  In the daily living;
Sometimes we forget
  We are to be forgiving.

Christmas can be
  Our only salvation;
We shed our hate
  Across the nation.

We feed the poor,
  The homeless, the ill;
Everyone seems to
  Be doing God's will.

We see the world
  Through the eyes of a child;
A baby named Jesus,
  So peaceful, so mild.

Let us look beyond
  This special season we love
And renew our faith
  In our God above.

9

Message of Love

Robert Colbert

Today I bring
  The message of love,
Of Christ who came
  From Heaven above.

New hope, new joy,
  He brings this morn.
Hallelujah! Praise God!
  Our King is born!

Joy and Peace

Cora M. Owen

Oh, what joy came to the earth,
At the time of Jesus' birth!
Angels told it. Shepherds heard
And to worship they were stirred.

Oh, what peace was brought to
  earth,
By that simple lowly birth,
On a night so calm and still,
Sheltered by Judean hill.

Christmas Is for Love

Marion Schoeberlein

Christmas is for happy hearts,
  Trees and wreaths and
    candlelight,
Families that kiss and hug,
  Memories that shine so bright.
Christmas is for little prayers,
  To God in Heaven above—
But most of all each Christmas is
  To make the world a place of love!

A Special Season

Helen Kitchell Evans

The Christmas season is special
  For Christians everywhere;
There's a special kind of feeling
  Fills the December air.

Our friends seem more friendly,
  Our food tastes special, too.
What can be the reason?
  Do you even have a clue?
    (Pause.)

You're right! It's all because
  Our Jesus came to earth;
And at this season every year
  We celebrate His birth.

Be Sure Jesus Shows

Helen Kitchell Evans

When we share our happiness
  Around a tree that glows,
Have we planned this celebration
  So that Jesus truly shows?

Let there be some symbol,
  A creche, a tiny rose—
Whatever is the custom
  But be sure that Jesus shows.

Make each Christmas celebration
  So the story each one knows;
Some place in the decorations
  Make sure that Jesus shows.

What I Wish

Cora M. Owen

I wish that I had seen the star
With wise men who had traveled
    far.
I wish that I had been with them,
When they came to Bethlehem.

I wish that I had worshiped there,
And seen the child that was so fair.
I wish that I had brought Him gold,
Myrrh, frankincense, like those of
    old.

Still

Cora M. Owen

Many years have come and gone,
Since the first great Christmas
    dawn;
Yet its message, ever sweet,
Christ is born! We still repeat.

Through the ages joy has rung.
Still the Christmas songs are sung.
Words announced by angel voice,
Still make hearts on earth rejoice.

Christmas Bells

Kay Hoffman

Ring out, O Christmas bells
    Across the world tonight;
Proclaim the holy Christ child's
    birth,
    God's gift of love and light.

Ring out the wondrous message
    O'er mansion and cottage small
"Unto us a Child is given,"
    A Savior born for all.

Above the shout of merry throngs,
    Above the world's loud din,
Ring out, O Christmas bells
    tonight,
    That hearts remember Him.

If I Had

Cora M. Owen

If I had followed that bright star,
That wise men saw in country far:
If I had come to Bethlehem,
And journeyed on the way with
    them;
If I had seen the baby fair,
I would have worshiped with them
    there,
And brought a gift so willingly.
The gift I gave would have been
    ME.

Christmas Morn

Lillian Robbins

The way I love my baby doll,
    (Holds doll.)
    And with her I always play,
I know I'd be happy to see
    Baby Jesus asleep on the hay.

But of course I couldn't be there
    Because I was not even born.
But now I can always celebrate
    On every Christmas morn.

Difficult

Busy Innkeeper?

Kay Hoffman

As Christmastime is here again
So many things come crowding in.
So much to plan, so much to do
The shopping days now but a few.

I walk through stores mid shopping
    throngs
Cash registers are sounding
    gongs.
I think about the crowded inn
(The keeper with "no room" for
    Him).

Midst tinseled scenes by crowds
    hemmed in
I yearn to see the stable dim.
It seems the Babe has been
    replaced
With Santa Claus' smiling face.

I hurry home with gifts to wrap
My strength and energy is
    strapped.
I search my heart and know it's true
I'm a busy innkeeper too.

OH, OH, OH, Christmas

Nell Ford Hann

Oh, Christmas!
  Hearts are bubbling with good
    cheer,
  Blessed, blissful time of year,
  As Jesus' birthday's drawing near,
OH . . . . OH . . . . OH, Christmas!

Oh, Christmas!
  Carolers' voices fill the air,
  Brotherhood of faith and care,
  Peace on earth . . . wished
    everywhere,
OH . . . . OH . . . . OH, Christmas!

Oh, Christmas!
  Children playing in the snow,
  To worship HIM in church . . . we
    go,
  'Tis the season we love so,
OH . . . . OH . . . . OH, Christmas!

Oh, Christmas!
  Children laughing with delight,
  Such a joyful, love-filled sight,
  Wondrous, glorious holy night,
OH . . . . OH . . . . OH, Christmas!

We Love Him So

Alta McLain

We can almost hear the angels sing
  Again this Christmas morn
Of Jesus, Son of God, with peace,
  Who in Bethlehem was born.

Shepherds in the night had heard,
  Believed, and went to see
A baby in a manger bed,
  The Prince of Peace to be.

Wise men knew, and followed
  A very lovely star,
And came to kneel before Him
  With love gifts from afar.

We, too, bring gifts, adore Him,
  And in our hearts we know
The Son of God is with us,
  And we love Him so.

Rejoicing Together

Alta McLain

We can be happy together
  On Christmas Day, for we know
God sent a wonderful baby
  To Bethlehem long ago.

Jesus was God's precious Son,
  A gift in deed of love.
A baby in a manger
  Brought joy from Heaven above.

He brought us peace, and wisdom,
  And truth that we might know
How to live, and serve Him,
  How to praise, and grow.

He answers all our questions.
  He's our hope for eternity,
And together we are rejoicing
  That love like this can be.

Wise Men Seek Jesus

Sharon Kaye Kiesel

We have come from afar, we kings of the East,
Following the star of the Prince of Peace.
We have read prophecies concerning the birth,
Of a new King who will rule the earth.

We have traveled long—are we too late?
As now we stand at Bethlehem's gate.
The star beam is low, we stand at its base,
Is this the house? Is this the place?

Where is this King, whose birth has come?
For we know surely He's an important Son.
A Lord to honor with our gifts from afar,
Oh where is this King? For we have seen His star.

Called From Heaven

Lillian Robbins

The journey was long,
　And Mary was tired
　When they came to Bethlehem.

The words rang loud
　In Joseph's ears,
　"No room for you in the inn!"

He knew that he must
　Find a place
　And bed where Mary could lay.

But the only spot
　Available to them—
　A stable where animals stay.

Joseph was honored
　To be the man
　Chosen as Mary's mate.

And with loving care
　He spread the hay.
　Not long did they have to wait.

The animals around
　Could not understand
　The strange events that night.

But a tiny babe
　Asleep in their trough
　Was surely a wonderful sight.

God's Son appeared,
　To earth He came,
　Born to a virgin maid.

Jesus was called
　From Heaven above,
　That folks could surely be saved.

I Lift Up My Eyes

Lillian Robbins

Lord, I lift my eyes up to You,
　My heart I open wide.
I thank You for Your blessings
　And know You're by my side.

I think of the baby Jesus
　As He lay in the manger bed,
And I see Your plan unfolding
　Just the way You always said.

I praise Your name forever
　For sending us Your Son,
Born in a lowly stable
　Your chosen anointed one.

As I celebrate this Christmas,
　I know it's filled with love
Because You sent the Savior
　From Heaven up above.

Thank You, Lord, for loving me
　And making salvation sure.
Because of Your son, Christ Jesus,
　Our trials we can all endure.

And now during the Christmas
　season
　I bow my head in prayer.
Thank You for always loving me
　Every moment, every day, every
　hour.

A Happy Christmas

Marion Schoeberlein

Families make a happy Christmas
And a bright Thanksgiving Day,
We laugh and eat and chat
   together,
We go to church and sing and pray,
Our hearts are thankful for the gifts
Of food and toys and clothing, too,
It's really God who gives it all—
No matter who gives things to
   you—
Of all the days in the whole year
Thanksgiving and Christmas are
   the best,
Because we are with family,
And Jesus is our special GUEST!

How Deep the Joy

Cora M. Owen

How deep the joy of angels' song,
   On that first Christmas night;
When they appeared to shepherds
   and
   The sky was filled with light.

How deep the joy that shepherds
   knew,
   As hurriedly they came,
To see the baby where He lay,
   And glorify His name.

How deep the joy that Mary felt,
   When that sweet babe was born.
She knew the Savior now had
   come,
   To bring a glad new morn.

How deep the joy when wise men
   found
   The precious Holy One;
Presented all their gifts so fine,
   To Jesus Christ, God's Son.

Bethlehem Star

Alyce Pickett

It's Christmas Eve and in the sky
   Millions of stars aglow
Shine as they did over Bethlehem
   That Christmas long ago.

I wonder, looking at one star . . .
   The brightest golden light,
If that could be the very one
   So many saw that night.

The bright one that the shepherds
   saw
   When they heard angels sing?
The same star that the magi used
   To find the Christ child-king?

Is that star staying now for us?
   Will it be shining when
Bright angels fill the sky with light,
   And Jesus comes again?

My New Year's Confession

Bob Wickline

Sure am glad the old year's passin',
And a new one is about to begin . . .
I pray I'll remember the lessons I've learned
And not make the same mistakes all over again.

But maybe with Jesus' help and guidance,
This year I'll do a little bit better . . .
Yet year-in and year-out I must confess
Before His grace I'm forever His debtor.

If we didn't learn it the hard way,
Don't suppose we'd learn it at all—
And we should be mighty thankful to the Lord
He's there to catch us when we fall.

Now, the Lord doesn't always expect us to win,
But He does expect us to try . . .
So keep on getting up when ya fall—
And **PRAY!** Never ever say die.

PRAY! Keep on strivin' to please the Lord,
And we'll get the hang of it by and by . . .
And when we finally make it to Heaven,
We can lay our burdens down,
And heave one heavenly SIGH . . .

"Not as though I had already attained, either were already perfect: but I follow after, if that I may apprehend that for which also I am apprehended of Christ Jesus. Brethren, I count not myself to have apprehended: but this one thing I do, forgetting those things which are behind, and reaching forth unto those things which are before, I press toward the mark for the prize of the high calling of God in Christ Jesus" (Philippians 3:12-14).

Exercises

Hang the Holly High

Helen Kitchell Evans

All:	Hang the holly wreath up high
	Where all may see as they pass by.
Child 1:	See the mistletoe and velvet bows,
Child 2:	See the lovely Christmas rose,
Child 3:	See the red poinsettia there,
Child 4:	Send the joy out everywhere,
Child 5:	Place within the wreath a dove,
Child 6:	Symbol of our Savior's love.
All:	Hang the holly wreath up high
	Where all may see as they pass by.

I Would Come

C. R. Scheidies

1: *(Holds picture of manger scene.)*
Into His presence, I would come today,
Worship at the manger, the Lord born in the hay.

2: *(Fold hands, bows head.)*
Humbly, like the Savior, I come in prayer,
For when I seek my Jesus, I always find Him there.

3: *(Holds cross.)*
The baby of the manger, is the Christ at Calvary,
Who gave His life that I might live, in resurrection victory.

4: *(Kneels.)*
So as I kneel this Christmas, I ask Jesus to come in,
Give Him my all, my hurts and sin, and, from this moment . . .
live for Him.

All: Into His presence, we come to worship and to praise,
Jesus, Savior, Lord of all, to Him our thanks we raise.

Song: "Joy to the World"

What Is Christmas?

Iris Gray Dowling

Child 1:	Christmas is a **joyful** time—
	Time to sing and say our rhymes.
Child 2:	Christmas is a time to know—
	God in Heaven **loves** us so.
Child 3:	Christmas is a time of **light**—
	Baby Jesus was born that night?
Child 4:	Christmas is a time for **peace**—
	When evil doesn't seem to cease.
Child 5:	Christmas is a time to live—
	Making others happy when we **give.**

*(To be recited by five children, each holding a card with the word
"CHRISTMAS" printed on one side and the bold word in their rhyme on
the other side. Words are: Joyful, Love, Light, Peace, Give. The word
CHRISTMAS could be printed in different colors for each child.
CHRISTMAS can be shown at the beginning of the exercise.)*

What Do We Love?

Helen Kitchell Evans

Child 1:	What do we love at Christmas?
All:	The gifts under the tree.
Child 2:	What do we love at Christmas?
All:	The Christmas lights we see.
Child 3:	What do we love at Christmas?
All:	The carols that we sing.
Child 4:	What do we love at Christmas?
All:	The joy that Christmas can bring.
Child 5:	What do we love at Christmas?
All:	The beautiful cards from friends.
Child 6:	What do we love at Christmas?
All:	The good food that never ends.
Child 7:	What do we love at Christmas?
All:	Most of all our Savior so dear.
Child 8:	What do we love at Christmas?
All:	The love that we feel to last all the year.

Christmas

Orpha A. Thomas

C is for the **Christ child** born in a manger bed.

H is for the **hay** on which He laid His head.

R is for the **ringing** of the bells on Christmas Day.

I is for the **innkeeper** that turned Jesus away.

S is for the **shepherds** that saw the shining stars.

T is for the **treasure** brought by wise men from afar.

M is for the **message:** words of wonder from above.

A is for the **angels** that sang of Jesus' love.

S is for **salvation;** that's why God's Son came.

Born on that first **Christmas. JESUS** is His name.

Jesus Came

Lillian Robbins

First Child:	Don't forget that Christmas Is the birthday of a king.
Second Child:	Wise men came to see Him, Their gifts to Him they bring.
Third Child:	Remember what the angel Told the shepherds on that night.
Fourth Child:	And the stars above the stable Were shining very bright.
Fifth Child:	The inn was way too crowded; They had no room for Him.
Sixth Child:	But now we know that Jesus Came to save us from our sin.

Christmas Comes and Christmas Goes

C. R. Scheidies

(For four children or groups: 1, 2, 3, 4)

1:   Christmas comes and Christmas goes,
2:   Gifts exchanged and then forgot,
(Pass wrapped boxes to 3 who holds them up.)
3:   But the gift that truly counts
4:   Is the gift of love that can't be bought.
(4: Hand over heart. 3: Places gifts at feet.)
All: "For God sent not his Son into the world to condemn the world; but that the world through him might be saved" (John 3:17).
1:   Angels heralded His birth,
3:   The majestic beings from on high,
(Raise one hand upward.)
2:   Sent lonely, smelly shepherds *(Hold nose.)*
4:   Who knelt His cradle by. *(Kneel, then rise slowly.)*
1 and 2: "For all have sinned, and come short of the glory of God" (Romans 3:23).
4:   Jesus brought love for each and every one.
3:   Compassion, joy, and peace.
2:   He came to give us life anew,
1:   And to die to set us free.
(All bow heads for a moment after last line.)
3 and 4: "For the wages of sin is death; but the gift of God is eternal life through Jesus Christ our Lord" (Romans 6:23).
(Each holds candle. Only one in each row is lit. As lights dim, those with lit candles light the candle of the one next to her and so on down the rows until all the candles are lit.)
2:   Yes, Christmas comes and Christmas goes,
4:   But the love of God remains
3.   To bring us light in a darkened world
1:   As we call upon His name.
All: "For God so loved the world, that he gave his only begotten Son, that whosoever believeth in him should not perish, but have everlasting life" (John 3:16).
4:   May you accept His gift today.
All: Merry CHRISTmas Day!
Song: "Thou Didst Leave Thy Throne"
    Verse one–1; Verse two–2 joins 1; Verse three–3 joins 1 and 2; Verse four–4 joins 1-3; Verse five–All

Happy Birthday Jesus!

Dixie Phillips

Each child should be holding a piece of poster board cut in half, with his letter written in dark bold lettering so the congregation can see them. The letters: HAPPY BIRTHDAY JESUS!

H - is for the hay they laid Him in that day.
A - is for the angel's song though King Herod meant Him wrong.
P - is for the people that came to the stall.
P - is for the peace He gave them when they gave their all.
Y - is for the year the Messiah came. Glory! Praise His holy name!

B - is for Bethlehem, the place of His birth.
I - am the reason He came to earth.
R - is for room. There was none in the inn.
T - is for the tidings: Good will toward men.
H - is for the heavenly host that filled the sky.
D - is for the donkey that carried Mary that night.
A - is for all. He will turn none away.
Y - is for you. Just accept Him today.

J - is for Joseph, His earthly father here.
E - is Emmanuel. We've nothing to fear.
S - is for the swaddling clothes Mary wrapped Him in.
U - is for the union, God with man.
S - is for our salvation, God's highest plan.

Smallest Child: Happy birthday Jesus!

(Teacher enters with a birthday cake with lit candles.)

Children Sing: Happy birthday to you.
Happy birthday to you.
Happy birthday dear Jesus
Happy birthday to you.

Now I Understand

Lillian Robbins

(An action poem for a young lady and a boy)

(Sitting at a table, Tom fiddles with a small toy while Mom writes a list.)

Tom: Mom, why do we talk about Christmas so much?
The calendar says it's months away.
Do I have to wait to get some toys
Just on Christmas day?

Mom: Certainly not, but that's a special day
We celebrate every year
To remember Jesus when He was born
And brought us all good cheer.

Tom: But does Jesus love us just one day?
Do you think that's true, dear Mom?

Mom: Of course not! Don't you know
What I always taught you, Tom?

Tom: You said always Jesus loves me
And He always cares for us.
But why not love Him every day
And not make such a fuss?

Mom: Well, it's just one day in all the year
When we remember His birth.
It's like our birth that we celebrate.
It's the day Jesus came to earth.

I'll stop writing my Christmas list,
And you come sit at my knee.
I guess it can be confusing to you
With all the things you see.

(Tom walks over and sits at Mom's feet.)

We talk so much about getting gifts
And giving some to our friends,
But always remember, it's all because
Of what Jesus did for men.

His great love caused Him to come
As a gift from God to man.
When we love God and follow His guide
We accept the gift He planned.

We surely love Jesus every day,
And Christmas is time we make
To celebrate the birth of Jesus our Lord
Who was born for all our sakes.

We accept His gift and give ourselves
When we listen and open our hearts.
We love and serve Him every day
If we just do our part.

Tom: I think I know what you're talking about.
Now I can understand.
Jesus is our gift, and we are His,
Every boy, girl, woman and man.

Happy Christmas Day, Mom!

(Tom gives Mom a hug.)

One Tiny Light

Sharon Kaye Kiesel

(Need five speakers, one soloist or song leader, four or more candlelighters, candles for all adult members of the congregation.)

First Speaker: In the beginning God's world was beautiful to behold,
Throughout creation His love ever flowed.
God walked with man in the garden's cool light,
Sharing joy and hope and there was no night.

Second Speaker: *(Room lights beginning a very slow dimming phase.)*
But Satan's greed destroyed this peace for men,
And man fell from God's grace—weighted by sin.
He was cast far beyond the garden gate,
Longing for God's presence, but it was too late.

(Room in darkness.)

Third Speaker: The sin and darkness grew as Satan's banner unfurled,
Evil, misery, sadness enveloped the world.
Men floundered, drowning in the sea of Satan's lies,
Always in fear for their mortal lives.

Fourth Speaker: God's love is so great and saddened by man's fall—
He sent His only Son, a light for us all.
From the manger, one tiny light began to glow *(First candle is lit.)*
And slowly from one to another the truth began to grow.

(Second, then third candles lit, fourth and then other candles lit and candlelighters move to the aisles, as fifth speaker recites. Other candles should then be lit as soloist sings.)

Fifth Speaker: Truth and hope spread quickly from one to another,
Through Jesus Christ we became sister and brother.
God's gift of light, fills our hearts with peace,
We are set free! From sin chains we are released.

Soloist: "O Come All Ye Faithful"

(By end of second verse most or all candles should be lit. All verses of song should be sung by congregation after soloist sings first verse. Impressive—on Chorus, first "let us adore him" is sung by soloist, second "let us" sung by children and youth, rest of chorus sung by entire congregation.)

How Can We "Not" Say Merry Christmas

Nell Ford Hann

How can we "not" say Merry Christmas,
  How can we leave one word out?
How can we pretend with "Season's Greetings"
  When Christ is what Christ-mas . . . . . is all about?

Christmas doesn't mean a store bought present,
  Though that is nice . . . when given from the heart,
Christmas doesn't mean ringing cash registers,
  And people tired from shopping 'til they drop.

Christmas doesn't mean festive parties,
  Or a December vacation . . . called Winter Holiday,
Christmas doesn't mean spending your last penny,
  To present a gift of silver or gold inlay.

Christmas does mean . . . gifts of joy and laughter,
  Friends . . . family . . . in unity, all over this earth,
Christmas means love and celebration . . . of
  Our blessed Savior, Jesus Christ's birth.

So how can we "not" say Merry Christmas?
  How can we leave one word out?
How can we just say "Season's Greetings,"
  When Christ is what Christ-mas is all about?

All Will Be Old Someday

Helen Kitchell Evans

Characters: Father; Mother; four children: Mike, Betty, Sam, Amy

Scene 1

The scene opens with the children talking.

Mike: With Christmas coming we should be thinking of what we can do for others.

Betty: Why is it you are so thoughtful of others? Why not something to make us feel good?

Sam: Betty, I can't believe you said that. Don't you ever learn anything at church?

Amy: She doesn't listen too well. Maybe that's her problem.

Betty: I do so listen. I like to make myself happy. Anything wrong with that? By the way, Mother says that Grandpa is going to be here for Christmas. Why do we always have to bother with him? There is always someone old to include. Why?

(Mother enters.)

Mother: What was that last question I heard you ask, Betty?

Betty: I asked, "Why do we always have to have Grandpa around?"

Mother: That's what I thought I heard. I'm glad your father isn't here to hear you say that. It would hurt him deeply.

Mike: Think of all the times he gave us gifts, took us places, and was always ready to take care of us when Mom and Dad were going to be gone for a few days.

Betty: Yeh, but that was before he was so old.

Sam: Don't you know that he doesn't enjoy being old, and trying to get along after that stroke? You will be old some day.

Betty: Me? Oh, I'll never be old and shuffle around like he does. He can't find anything. He's always asking for help in finding his hat, his glasses and—

Mother: Oh yes, you will get old. Grandpa was an active man. That stroke really changed him. I think you and perhaps all of us need a visit to the nursing home this afternoon. Today is open house for visitors to talk with assigned patients.

Betty: Oh no!
Mother: Oh yes! You especially, Betty, need to go. Get ready.

(They leave.)

Scene 2

Family is gathered around the dinner table. Father is present, too.

Father: Why is everyone quiet? Your mother says you did a good deed this afternoon.
Betty: Yes, we went to the nursing home.
Sam: Each of us talked to a different person for about fifteen minutes. Then we all got together and sang Christmas carols.
Amy: It was quite an experience.
Mike: You can say that again.
Amy: It really made me appreciate being young and able to get around so easily.
Father: That's good. Now you see why we are trying to give Grandpa as much attention as possible. We want to keep him in his own home as long as we can.
Betty: Mother says that he is coming for Christmas. Well, you had better believe that this year I'll try extra hard to be kind to him.

(A long silence, all look at Betty.)

Father: Why so silent? Why are you looking at Betty?
Mother: I think the children saw another side of life today. They learned everyone is valuable, useful, and important to God.
Betty: I sure did. I also learned you get back exactly what you give. Today I gave love and tonight I feel love. The lady I visited used to be a teacher. She told me how she loved to teach children, then became ill and could not live alone any more. She asked me to come back and visit her again.
Mother: And will you go?
Betty: Indeed I will.
Father: Sounds to me as though the Christmas spirit arrived at our house this afternoon.

(All leave stage.)

Mr. Carroll's Christmas

Alyce Pickett

This play's action takes place in three scenes, but is easy to produce. The props for two scenes are identical, and little change is required for the third scene. A curtain is needed, and a piano is desirable if one of the children can play the Christmas songs.

Characters: Mrs. Slater—in charge of Christmas program.
Tom Slater—her son.
Reba Slater—her daughter.
Jerry, Wayne, Jeff, Mary, Sally—5th or 6th grade children.
Mr. Carroll—a retired teacher.
3 or 4 Adults—residents of retirement home.

Props: Scenes 1 and 2, the Slaters' family room, use usual den furniture. A window at one end of room. Piano, if available. Rearrange same furniture for lobby of a retirement home for scene 3. Sofa or chair covers may be used to give the room a different appearance.

Time: The present. A few days before Christmas.

Costumes: Casual attire.

Scene 1

A knock is heard at the door. Tom puts his book on the table and goes to welcome his friend Jerry. Boys exchange greetings.

Tom: You're the first one here for practice.

(Both boys move near the window and look out on the street.)

Jerry: Look at that poor old man in the street!
Tom: Poor nothing! That's a staggering drunk.
Jerry: How do you *know*?

Tom: My brother told me about them. He says they stay on the streets and beg, then buy whiskey with the money they get. They stagger back to the shelter to get food, and so they'll be warm at night.

Jerry *(excitedly):* Let's follow him and see where he goes.

Tom: Okay. *(Boys hurry out.)*

(Mary, Jeff, Wayne, Sally, and Reba enter, talking.)

Mary: Anybody know where Tom and Jerry are?

Others: *(Shake heads or say no.)*

Jeff: They were supposed to meet us here.

Sally: Yeah, but where are they? *(Children talk together.)*

Reba: My brother is always late. Let's practice a song while we wait.

(Children sing two stanzas of a Christmas song.)

Wayne: Maybe we ought to call and see if we can find our missing members.

(Tom and Jerry enter, out of breath.)

Jeff: What happened to you? We've been waiting for hours. *(Looks at watch.)* Well—for half an hour.

Tom: We followed an old man who was staggering to see if he was a drunk going to a shelter.

Reba: Tom! You know you're not supposed to go near a drunk person.

Jerry: We didn't . . . I mean he wasn't drunk at all. We followed him for three blocks and then . . . he fell . . .

Mary: He fell? What did you do then?

Tom: We ran up to him and asked if he was hurt and asked if we could help him.

Jerry: We picked up the papers and bag of candy he dropped, and just stayed with him until help came.

Tom *(grinning):* The ambulance driver asked us if the man was our grandfather.

Jerry: We thought he was a drunk because he staggered, but he was just real old and weak. He told us his name is Bob Carroll.

Sally: Was the old man hurt?

Tom: Yeah, I think he broke his ankle. His foot looked twisted, and he said it hurt. The ambulance took him to the hospital.

Jerry: When the men were putting him on the little carrier thing, he smiled at us and said, "Thanks fellows." He's nice.

Tom: I wish we could visit him in the hospital. *(pause)* Maybe Mom would call and see if he's all right, and we might go see him.

Reba: We'll ask her when she gets back from the store.

Mary: I think we should practice now. *(Children move around piano.)*

Scene 2

Children and Mrs. Slater are in the same room, talking.

Tom: Will you do it, Mom? Will you call the hospital?

Mrs. Slater: All right, all right. I'll phone and see if they'll tell me anything about Mr. Carroll. But you won't be able to visit in the hospital, because you're too young. *(Exit.)*

Wayne: Why do hospitals have unfair rules like that? What's wrong with twelve-year-olds visiting in a hospital?

Sally: They might be sick and spread germs, or get in the way.

Jeff: That's silly. Older people have as many germs as we do.

Reba: Maybe you should tell them that. I bet they have some good reasons, though.

Mrs. Slater *(enters):* Mr. Carroll is 80 years old, a retired teacher. He lives in the retirement home on Anders Avenue, and he's back there now with his foot in a cast.

Children: May we go there to see him?

Mrs. Slater: Well, not today.

Tom: Tomorrow? May we go tomorrow?

Mrs. Slater *(hesitates):* I don't know. I'll call and see if it's possible.

Child: Thank you, thank you.

Mrs. Slater *(turns back at door):* I have a suggestion: Why don't you practice your program now and, if we do go tomorrow, you might sing your songs for Mr. Carroll and the others there.

Child: Great! Let's practice. *(All move to piano area.)*

Scene 3

Furniture rearranged to appear different from the previous scenes. Mr. Carroll and three friends are in the room when the others enter.

Tom: Hello, Mr. Carroll. *(Shakes his hand.)* I hope you feel better today. This is my mother, Mrs. Slater, and my friends.

(All shake hands with him. The children tell their names, shake hands with other adults.)

Mr. Carroll: Yes, I'm much better. *(Smiles.)* I surely was glad to see you boys yesterday when I fell. I tried to walk too far and couldn't make it back. I must be getting old *(Nods toward other adults.)* like my friends.

Mrs. Slater: We're glad you don't have to be in the hospital for Christmas. We wondered if you'd like us to sing some of the carols we've been practicing?

Mr. Carroll *(and others):* Oh yes, yes.

(Children sing "Silent Night," "Hark! the Herald Angels Sing," and "We Wish You a Merry Christmas" or other substitutions. Mrs. Slater takes gifts from shopping bag and gives one to each resident as the children are finishing the last song.)

Jerry: We hope your foot will soon be good as new, Mr. Carroll.

Mr. Carroll: Thank you. You'll all come again, won't you?

(Children look at Mrs. Slater.)

Mrs. Slater: We surely will. I promise. Happy holidays.

(All say good-byes.)

The Best Gift

Carol Hillebrenner

A multigenerational Christmas play

Cast:

Grandparent	Prophet Isaiah	Angel
Mary	Joseph	Three Kings
Children	Choir	

Props: Large chair, manger and baby doll, some low stools, costumes for seven Biblical characters, some tall stools, electrically lit star suspended from ceiling (opt.), king's three gifts, collection plates *(possibly stored under manger)*

Stage: Any raised area with tall stools behind large chair and shorter stools to either side of it, but not all the children will have stools to sit on. Manger should be stage center with short stools for Mary and Joseph to either side of it. Be certain kneeling children aren't hidden by manger.

Suggestions: The grandparent and Biblical characters may be played by teenagers.

Narrator (*enter*): Welcome everyone to the Christmas play entitled *The Best Gift.*

Grandparent enters with children. Grandparent takes the big chair. A small (quiet) child may sit on his lap. Other children sit on stools or stand behind stools and some may kneel or sit around grandparent's chair if they can be seen.

Grandparent: That turkey sure smells good. I'm glad dinner is almost ready.

Child 1: Tell us a story, Grandpa(ma).

(Other children nod. Others say something like, "Yes, tell us a story.")

Grandparent: Good idea. Would you like to hear a Christmas story?

Child 2: Will it be about Santa?

Grandparent: No, this is a true story about Christmas. It's about a gift, the very best gift ever.

Child 3: Did someone find it under a Christmas tree?

Grandparent: No, it was a better place than that.

Child 4: Was it a surprise gift?

Grandparent: No, people waited hundreds of years for this gift. A long, long time ago there were people called prophets. They told people about the special gift they would receive. The prophet Isaiah told them what the gift would be like.

(Enter Prophet Isaiah.)

Prophet: "For unto us a child is born, unto us a son is given: and the government shall be upon his shoulder: and his name shall be called Wonderful, Counselor, The mighty God, The everlasting Father, The Prince of Peace" (Isaiah 9:6).

(Exit Prophet Isaiah.)

Child 5: That sounds like somebody really important.

Grandparent: Yes, He was very important. His story begins more than two thousand years ago.

Child 6: That is a long time. Were you there when the gift came Grandpa?

Grandparent: No, it was a long time before even I was born and it arrived on the other side of the world. Have you guessed what the gift was?

Children *(in unison)*: The baby Jesus!

Grandparent: Yes, the baby Jesus was the gift. Long before he arrived the prophet Micah said where the baby Jesus would be born. Do you remember the name of that town?

Children *(in unison)*: Bethlehem!

Grandparent: Right, and we know a song about Bethlehem, don't we. Let's sing it together.

(Children sing first verse of "O Little Town of Bethlehem" with support of choir.)

Grandparent: Two thousand years ago a young woman named Mary and her husband Joseph arrived in Bethlehem after a long journey. They tried to find a place to sleep for the night, but all the rooms in the inns were full of other travelers. There was simply no place to stay except a stable. There they found straw to sleep on, a roof over their heads, and animals to help keep them warm. And it was a quieter place than the inn, but, you know, a stable is really a kind of barn. Would you expect to find someone called the Prince of Peace in a barn?

Children: No! *(Not in unison and some should just wag heads.)*

Grandparent: But that's exactly what happened. While Joseph and Mary were in the stable, Mary gave birth to baby Jesus. Now this baby wasn't just any baby. This baby was the best gift ever given to the world.

(Enter Mary and Joseph, Mary carrying blanket-wrapped doll. Mary lays doll in manger and they both sit down.)

Mary: Isn't he a beautiful baby? The angel said we should name him Jesus. That's a good name, isn't it?

Joseph: Yes, it is a good name for the Son of God, but this stable is a strange place for our future king to be born. I must say I don't understand God's plan.

Children *(with support of choir sing):* "Away in a Manager"

Child 7: Did other people learn about the wonderful gift, Grandpa?

Grandparent: They sure did and in a really special way. The first to hear the good news were some shepherds out watching their flocks, protecting the sheep from hungry bears and wolves. It was a quiet night until, suddenly, an angel appeared in the sky.

(Enter Angel.)

Angel: Don't be afraid. I have good news for you. This very night a baby has been born in Bethlehem. This baby is the promised Messiah. He has come to save all people.

Choir: "Joy to the World"

(Exit Angel.)

Child 8: Are those the only people who knew that baby Jesus was born?

Grandparent: No, most people knew something really remarkable was happening because a huge star appeared in the sky. It shone over the place where Jesus was born. *(Turn on star prop if available. Grandparent and children look up at star briefly.)* A long way to the east of Bethlehem there were wise men who studied the stars. When they saw this wonderful new star, they started west as fast as they could to find out what it meant.

(Enter three kings who kneel by manger and present their gifts to Mary and Joseph.)

Choir: "We Three Kings of Orient Are"

Child 9: That's a great story, Grandpa. I'm glad it's a true story.

Child 10: Is that why we receive gifts at Christmas, so we won't forget that God gave us the first and best gift?

Grandparent: Yes, we receive and give gifts as symbols of the greatest gift.

(Offering may be taken up at this point if so desired. Joseph and kings or older children may take offering. During the offering the congregation may sing "Watchman, Tell Us of the Night" or "It Came upon the Midnight Clear" or "Good Christian Men, Rejoice" or some other selection.)

Child 11: Will you tell us more stories about Jesus, Grandpa?

Grandparent: I'd be happy to. Telling people about Jesus is what being part of Jesus' family is all about. We never want to forget about the best gift.

(Enter older child.)

Older Child: Dinner is ready. Did Grandpa tell you a Christmas story?

Child 12: Yes, he told us the best story of all, the story about the best gift of all.

Older Child: And what is the best gift?

Children: The baby Jesus!

Grandparent *(arises and signals children and congregation to arise also):* While we're all here as a family, let's sing one more song together. *(Sing "Joy to the World" or "Silent Night" or some other favorite selection.)*

Narrator: Thank you for coming (and any other messages).

Christmas Guests

Dixie Phillips

The Narrator may be played by either an adult or an older child dressed up as his Sunday school teacher would.

Props: Manger scene.

Narrator: We'd like to take this time to welcome each one of you to our Christmas program today. My name is _____. We are very fortunate to have some special Christmas guests with us today. Why— I've seen a few shepherds, some wise men, and even several angels right here in this sanctuary. Look! *(Point toward children.)* Here comes a shepherd now.

Shepherd #1: *(Carrying stuffed toy lamb.)*
Have you seen the Messiah?
I heard that He came.
They say if you see Him.
You will never be the same.

Shepherd #2: *(Carrying a staff.)*
Have you seen the Messiah?
God's special Holy One.
He's the reason why—
I have come.

(After shepherds say their lines they should go and stand near the manger.)

Narrator: It was very exciting the night Jesus was born. There was a bright star shining in the east.

(Child enters with a star mask. Only her face peering through. Special effects—glow-in-the-dark costume.)

Star: I am the star that shone so bright!
   I lit up the sky that holy night!

Narrator: The wise men followed the star to where the Baby lay.

(Wise men enter one at a time.)

Wise man #1: I am a wise man as you can see.
   So I worship on bended knee. *(Present gift.)*

Wise man #2: To you little king, of whom I've been told,
   I present my gift of gold. *(Present gift.)*

Wise man #3: I humbly bow before my King.
   My gift of frankincense I bring. *(Present gift.)*

(Wise men kneel around manger.)

Narrator: I think I see *(Cupping hands over squinting eyes.)* a heavenly
   host.

Angels: *(unison)*
   When we heard *(cup ear)* of His birth
   We flew *(flap wings)* quickly to earth.
   What news do we bring? *(palms up)*
   To you *(point)* is born the King of kings!

Narrator: We are so blessed to have with us today—Mary, the mother of
   this tiny baby Jesus. Let's listen to what she has to say.

Mary: Shhhhh! He's sleeping so very peacefully.
   Why, He's the cutest baby, I ever did see.
   We've had a busy day, *(Wipe brow.)*
   So many guests came our way.
   They all say He is a Special One!
   I know it is true for He is God's Son.

(Mary sits next to manger, looking lovingly at the Baby.)

Narrator: Look! Joseph has come to honor us with his presence.

Joseph: Did you see His tiny hands?
  They will bleed one day for man.
  Did you see His perfect little head?
  One day, His blood will be shed.
  What perfect little feet.
  It will not end in defeat.
  For God has sent His Son.
  Because He loves us everyone!

(Joseph stands behind Mary. Children should be standing to create a nativity scene.)

Children *(sing):* "Away in a Manger"

Help Others on Thanksgiving

Lillian Robbins

The Pilgrims had corn and turkey that was wild,
  And we have turkey, too.
The Children of Israel ate lamb and herbs,
  Their feast honored God, it's true.

No matter how people celebrate a day,
  The reason is the important thing.
We open our hearts and thank the Lord
  And glory to His name we bring.

On the calendar, this day comes once a year,
  But people should always know,
Every day we thank the Father above,
  Our respect and love we show.

So today as we share with those we love,
  In pleasure and tremendous joy,
Why not remember those in need.
  Help families and girls and boys.

The Lord Jesus taught us to care and share
  When He was here on earth,
And to spend a godly Thanksgiving Day,
  Let's remember to help others first.

Thanksgiving

How I'll Prove It

Margaretta Harmon

How can I prove that I'm thankful
For Jesus, who came from above?
I'll tell Him each day
In the prayers that I say,
And I'll show Him by kindness and
    love.

A Thought for Thanksgiving

Margaretta Harmon

God bless us the whole year
    through.
I thank Him every day. Do you?

Now's the Time

Margaretta Harmon

Once more it's Thanksgiving Day,
And time for all of us to say,
"We thank you, Lord, in every
    way."

In His Name

Rega Kramer McCarty

Welcome to you all today,
    We are so glad you came.
Let us give our thanks to God
    And pray in Jesus' name.

Thanks to God

Mary Howard Poole

I'm glad we have a special day
On which we meet to gladly say
Our thanks to God for homes and
    health,
For land so blest with freedom's
    wealth.

We Offer Thanks

Mary Howard Poole

For loving family and friends,
For food from sea and sod,
For every gift your goodness
    sends
We give you thanks, dear God.

40

Thanksgiving Greeting

Margaretta Harmon

Come, ye thankful people, come;
Let's praise Jesus, everyone!

Thanksgiving Day

Helen Kitchell Evans

Thanksgiving's the day
   For family and friends;
A home filled with joy
   That never ends.

A home where all know
   Love and sharing;
A home where all
   Will know abundant caring.

I'm Thankful

Orpha A. Thomas

I'm thankful for my dear daddy
   And for my mommy so sweet,
For my soft warm bed at night,
   And the yummy food I eat.
I'm thankful that Jesus loves me.
   That He takes care of me each
   day.
And that He listens and answers
And always hears when I pray.

Thanks, Lord

Phyllis C. Michael

Thank You, Lord, for Thanksgiving
   Day
   The time when we pause to
   remember
All of the blessings You've sent our
   way
   January through December.

I could mention a thousand things
   and one
   I'm truly thankful for.
But then I know I'd never get done
   There would always be one more
Just waiting to be named like all
   the rest.
   There's my family, and oh, yes,
   my good friends
And all of the things we like to do
   best—
   The list just never ends.

So thank You, Lord, for
   Thanksgiving Day
   And help us never forget
We can thank You best in work or
   play
   By never doing things we'll
   regret.

Best of Holidays

Helen Kitchell Evans

Somebody asked me to state
  Why I like the Thanksgiving
    season;
Well,—I confess it is good to eat
  But that's not the entire reason.

It's because it reminds all of us
  How fortunate we are;
Lots of food and lots of clothes
  And a brand new family car.

So many things to be thankful for,
  So much in life to praise;
Today is one great time of year,
  The best of holidays.

Today Is My Thanksgiving Day

Helen Kitchell Evans

Today is my Thanksgiving Day
  A day to sing out praise
For all the blessings that are mine
  Given to me in so many ways.

For the beautiful world in which I
    live,
  For the midnight sky and the
    moon's soft glow,
For the fields of waving grain
  That cover this earth below.

Yes, today is my Thanksgiving Day,
  A time to return a part of such love
That can only be given by one—
  Our Savior in Heaven above.

In Each Heart

Helen Kitchell Evans

Let us be thankful for sunshine
  And the beauty of the sky
When the colors of the sunset
  Gently fade away on high.

Let us be thankful for kindly smiles
  Given to us by our friends;
Let us be very grateful
  For God's love that never ends.

This is a time for Thanksgiving.
  One day each year set apart
To truly give praise for all blessings
  So let love abound in each heart.

Every Day Thanksgiving

Helen Kitchell Evans

So often we accept our blessings
  Without a word of praise,
A cheerful, friendly greeting
  Or a hug on rainy days.

Some unexpected kindness
  From a stranger on our way.
A spoken word of hope
  By a friend who came to say,
"You know I'm here to help,
  To offer up a prayer,
Anything you ask I'll do
  For you know I truly care."

Let us pause for blessings given
  And for each day of living,
Let's vow to fill our lives with praise
  And make every day
    Thanksgiving.

I'm Thankful

Kay Hoffman

I'm thankful for so many things
  On this Thanksgiving Day;
I'm thankful for this land I love
  Where I may kneel and pray.

For sunshine warm and gentle
  rain,
  For flowers, birds and trees,
For friendship true and family ties,
  I offer thanks for these.

For golden yield of fruit and grain,
  The harvest gathered in
I'm thankful for the ample share
  In larder, mow and bin.

And now as we assemble
  Around the festive board,
I'm thankful for each loved one
  here
  And for your presence Lord!

Harvest Prayer

Kay Hoffman

The harvest season's over;
  The yield is gathered in;
God in His tender mercy
  Has blessed us once again.

Vegetables and fruit and grain
  Are heaped high everywhere,
Enough to see the winter through
  And still enough to share.

As God has blessed our harvest,
  It's only right that we should give
To those who are less fortunate,
  Wherever they may live.

As we give thanks at table grace,
  O may we humbly pray
That none would have an empty
  plate
  On this Thanksgiving Day.

43

Giving Thanks

Alyce Pickett

I wonder when God made the stars
 If He counted every one,
Or if He just said the right word
 And all, at once, were done?

And how about the other things?
 Did He just speak a wish
To make all different kinds of birds
 And animals and fish?

Did He say, "Plants," and suddenly
 There were millions of these . . .
Fruits, vegetables, and flowers . . .
 And all the kinds of trees?

No one but God had power to
 make
 All of the things we see;
And He's the only one who'd know
 How all things ought to be.

That's why I'm thanking Him today
 For all the things He's done
To make our world, then make us,
 too,
 And love us, every one.

I Want To Be Like You

Lillian Robbins

Thank You, Lord, for little things
 Like kittens and puppies and
 birds,
For sunshine and flowers and
 swimming pools
 And music that's always heard.

Help me, Lord, to remember
 How You give me life and love
And never ever forsake me
 But watch me from up above.

Teach me, Lord, to be loving
 And kind to all I know,
To try to treat all others
 With love like You do show.

Forgive me, Lord, when I fail You,
 Forget to help the poor,
Or complain 'bout things not
 worthy.
 You can touch my heart I'm sure.

Show me, Lord, how to thank You
 For all You do for me.
Give me hope and peace while I'm
 growing
 Like You I want to be.

Give thanks

A Thanksgiving Psalm

Dorothy M. Page

This program can be used in several ways. A group of five persons, all female, all male, or mixed; costumed, or in street dress. This program can also use three speakers and all three recite the last two verses in chorus.

Speaker #1:
For our parents' loving care,
For the Christian home we
     share,
For the prayers we all learned
     there,
     Father we thank Thee.

Speaker #2:
For a spouse loving and true,
For a love that grew and grew,
For the vows we now renew,
     Father we thank Thee.

Speaker #3:
For our children ever dear,
For the friends who are sincere,
For warmth, and joy, and cheer,
     Father we thank Thee.

Speaker #4:
For the music we can hear,
For eyes to see skies bright
     and clear,
For the beauty of our sphere,
     Father we thank Thee.

Speaker #5:
For the knowledge thou art
     near,

For release from doubt and fear,
For Thy peace through sorrow's
     tear,
     Father we thank Thee.

Let's all give thanks

For All

Helen Kitchell Evans

Choir 1:	The harvest is in
Choir 2:	To fill our need;
Choir 1:	God gave to us
Choir 2:	From a tiny seed.
Choir 1:	The lovely fruits,
Choir 2:	Vegetables and meat;
Chorus:	Thank God for food,
	Good things to eat.
Solo 1:	Upon this day of feast
	and prayer
Solo 2:	We gather now with
	God to share
	Our thanks for
	blessings we recall
Chorus:	For home, for family,
	yes, for all.

45

Thanks Again

Alta McLain

We thank You, Father, once again
For all the good things that have been,
   For home, and church, and family, friends,
   For hope that on your love depends.
Thank You for filling every need,
For Your Word that we can read,
   For the beauty of the earth,
   For special favors from our birth.
Thanks Father for your precious Son
Who lived, and died for everyone.
   We know He'll not forsake us here,
   That perfect love casts out fear.

Daily Thanksgiving

Alyce Pickett

We talked about Thanksgiving at church today, and everybody had some things they could name that made them happy. Some of us could be thankful for hundreds of things.

Then Todd told us about many, many more. Todd's awfully smart. He said we should be thankful for millions of stars, and because God made them so they'd stay in place and shine and not bump together and fall on us. Then he talked about the plants and trees, the different birds and all kinds of animals and fish.

"Of course we're thankful *for all of them,*" we told Todd.

"We have to be *real* thankful for God, and that He knows everything," Todd said then. "S'pose somebody else had tried to make the earth? They might have made fields of red grass and made red trees that would make your eyes tired. They might not have made cows to give milk for children or any plants to get sugar from or anything good to eat."

Then I told Todd something. "Don't worry about it," I said. "Nobody else would have power to make a tree of *any* color, or anything else. Only God had the power to make things like that, and He made everything *right* 'cause He knew how things *ought to be.*"

We decided we should thank God often all during the year for making the earth . . . and everything in it . . . and for making and loving us.

A Litany of Praise

Faye Nyce

First Person: "Give thanks to the Lord, for he is good. His love endures forever" (Psalms 136:1).

Second Person: Just as He forgave the children of Israel many times, so He often forgives me.

Third Person: "Praise the Lord, O my soul; all my inmost being, praise his holy name" (Psalm 103:1).

Fourth Person: How can I so easily forget to praise Him? Why do I have to search for reasons to thank Him? Without Him I would not have my next breath. Without Him there would be no tomorrow—nor even today!

All: "Sing to the Lord a new song, for he has done marvelous things" (Psalm 98:1).

First Person: I praise and thank Him for strength and health; for His dependability—that day follows night; that He knew just how far to put the sun from the earth; for the perfection of the universe.

Fifth Person: "Come, let us sing for joy to the Lord; let us shout aloud to the Rock of our salvation. For the Lord is the great God, the great King above all gods" (Psalm 95:1, 3).

Sixth Person: I come to You, Lord, admitting that many times other things come before You in my life. I do not always leave room for You to be that great King above all gods. Yet I must acknowledge that You truly are the rock of my salvation. "In you, O Lord, I have taken refuge" (Psalm 71:1).

Second and Fifth Persons: "God is our refuge and strength," (Psalm 46:1a) always present whether in trouble or jubilation. We need not fear, though there are wars, earthquakes, floods, storms of all kinds, or illness.

All: Yet we are human—these things do frighten us. They shake our security.

Third Person: But we can be thankful—we know "the Lord Almighty is with us; the God of Jacob is our fortress" (Psalm 46:7).

Fourth Person: "Many, O Lord my God, are the wonders you have done. The things you planned for us no one can recount to you; were I to speak and tell of them, they would be too many to declare" (Psalm 40:5).

Sixth Person: Yet I want to declare to all who hear me that the God of Heaven is my Lord. He is merciful to me; He has redeemed me by sending His son; I can look forward to a home in Heaven.

First Person: I declare my thankfulness for my church family. Though none of us is perfect, we are traveling the road together, upholding each other in crises and rejoicing with one another in times of blessing.

Second Person: I declare my thankfulness for my mother and father—they show me love and patience in so many ways. They have supplied my earthly needs.

Fifth Person: I declare my thankfulness for my grandparents, aunts and uncles. The strength of our shared relationship is like a firm pillar to me.

Second and Third Persons: We declare our thankfulness for our community—thankful that we can sleep at night without fear of bombs dropping in our town, without fear of enemies breaking down the front door, without fear of any kind of disturbance.

Fourth Person: I declare my thankfulness for enough to eat. Though we may complain about rising prices, our cupboards are never bare. We know where our next meal is coming from.

Sixth Person: I declare my thankfulness that I can read. It is a gift to be able to expand my mind by reading what others have written, and learning about other people in other places and times.

Second Person: I declare my thankfulness for my friends and what they have contributed to my life.

Third Person: I declare my thankfulness that people all though the ages were faithful in passing on the good news of Jesus Christ, some even risking their lives to preserve the Word of God.

All: "Give thanks to the Lord, for he is good. His love endures forever!" (Psalm 136:1).

Fourth Person: I declare my thankfulness for the beauty of the natural world:

Fifth Person: . . . the song of the robin,

Sixth Person: . . . the flight of a butterfly,

Third Person: . . . the bountiful harvest,

Second Person: . . . the majesty of the mountains,

Fourth Person: . . . the shimmering red leaves of the maple tree,

First Person: . . . the brilliance of a full moon,

Fifth Person: . . . the gleaming of the stars,

Third Person: . . . the splash of the waves at the seashore,

Second Person: . . . the golden fields of grain.

First and Fourth Persons: When we stop to count all your good works, O God, they are more than can be numbered. We are filled with awe!

All: "Give thanks to the Lord, for he is good. His love endures forever!" (Psalm 136:1).

All Scriptures from the *Holy Bible, New International Version.*